A LETTER

TO

THE EDITOR OF THE COLOMBO OBSERVER

On Temperance Societies.

~~~~~~~~

BY THE SENIOR COLONIAL CHAPLAIN OF THE

ISLAND OF CEYLON.

He who freely magnifies what hath been nobly done, and fears not to declare as freely what might be done better, gives ye the best covenant of his fidelity; and that his loyalest affection and his hope waits on your proceeding. His highest praising is not flattery, and his plainest advice is a kind of praising.

MILTON'S AREOPAGITICA.

COLOMBO:

PRINTED AT THE WESLEYAN MISSION PRESS.

1835.

To

THE HONORABLE

MAJOR GENERAL

SIR JOHN WILSON

COMMANDER OF THE FORCES.

&c.   &c.   &c.

Sir,

Although the following Pamphlet is written in the form of a letter, and was first intended for the columns of a News paper; yet, as it is now an entirely separate Publication, I apprehend that there can be no impropriety in my desire to inscribe it to You. You, Sir, are the Commander of His Majesty's Forces in this Colony. As such, you are most deeply interested in the bodily health and the moral wellbeing of the Troops under your Command. It is on their account only, as their Chaplain at this station, that I have taken any part in the question of Temperance Societies. It is on their account that I now request to place your Name at the head of these remarks. If without danger of plunging them further into sin, by the breach of that Declaration or Vow, which, as these societies are now constituted, every member is required to sign; if some common principle can be found, upon which they can be safely introduced among our fine Soldiery, who are daily, nay hourly, destroying body and soul by the abhorrent habit of spirit-drinking, it were indeed, Sir, "a consummation devoutly to be wished."

The circumstance, which compels me to adopt this form of publication, is the avowed inability of the Editor of the Colombo Observer to insert it in his columns. I have, however, the greatest pleasure in giving publicity to an offer of the Editor, not only to print the letter in the present form of a Pamphlet, at his own press, but to bear an equal share in the necessary expenses. If the offer have been declined, it has not been without the fullest sense of the right feeling which dictated that offer.

The Editor of the Colombo Observer has stated that I " feel compelled publicly to record my sentiments on a subject connected with morals and agitated in all ranks of society." This is not quite correct. The motive, which has induced me to come forward,—a motive which absorbs all others,—is, as I have already stated, my being the Chaplain of this principal station of the island. I have, moreover, felt myself called upon by the Editor, and by his correspondents: and that I might not lie under the imputation of indifference to the moral wellbeing of my fellow creatures, especially in Colombo, I have not shrunk from this unenviable duty.

And now, Sir, ere I take my leave, permit me to state, that, since the appearance of a most unworthy attack upon you by an anonymous Correspondent of the Colombo Observer, I have taken the liberty to inquire into your connection with the Troops under your command in this island. The result is indeed most triumphant as regards Yourself,—most gratifying to your numerous friends,—and most satisfactory to all honorable minds. I find that the Name of MAJOR GENERAL SIR JOHN WILSON stands at the head of Benefactors of the Troops personally,— stands higher than any of his gallant predecessors, as the *tried, faithful, and kind* FRIEND OF THE PRIVATE SOLDIER!! I find that, for many and substantial comforts to which the *soldier* has been heretofore a stranger, he is indebted, and he gratefully feels that he is indebted, to the present Commander of the Forces. I find this result attested by those who have known the Colony for upwards of twenty years. Any malignant endeavour, therefore,

Sir, to lessen your high character by anonymous slander will be treated by You, and by all men of upright feeling, with merited contempt. The calumniator "bites on the file" of public reprobation, and, I trust, of self-condemnation.

My situation necessarily precludes me from the possible imputation of any interested or unworthy motive in this public avowal of my feelings: I am but paying honor and justice where honor and justice are due: and I rejoice in the opportunity of thus openly and unreservedly expressing my own grateful sense of your uniform courtesy, and of your personal kindness to myself individually.

I have the honor to remain,

With the highest feelings of respect and regard,

Sir,

Your most faithful, and obedient Servant,

B. BAILEY.

Colombo. September 29. 1835.

LETTER.

&c.   &c.   &c

TO THE EDITOR OF THE COLOMBO OBSERVER.

SIR,

Permit me to express to you, thus publicly, my thanks for the small, but important, Tracts with which you have obliged me, respecting the Temperance Societies. Through yourself and and your correspondents you have, in a few short weeks, introduced these societies to the hopes and the wishes, and, in some instances perhaps, to the good humoured smiles, of the Public of Colombo. Of these Tracts, and the *Declaration* that accompanies them, I shall presently speak. I will first mention the mode in which this subject has been introduced to my own notice, and subsequently to that of the society in this place, and touched and generalized, not closely grappled with, in your columns.

About twelve months since I received some documents, through the Assistant Military Secretary, from the Major General Commanding the Forces, touching a Temperance Society, which was proposed by the Chaplain of Galle; and with reference to the feasibility of its extension to the Maritime Capital. Temperance Societies have sprung up since I left England; and my answer was that I had not turned my attention to them: and the matter, so far as I was concerned in it, dropped. My notion of these societies at that time was vague and general. I thought, in common with many others, that,—in this age, when the intemperance of the common people, especially of the soldiery, had arrived at "such a *pernicious* height," and the evil was felt and acknowledged by all,—there must be "something rotten in the state of Denmark," to excite, and to sustain the opposition and ridicule which the friends of these societies so studiously endeavoured to ward off. I confess, on closer inspection, that I think so still. To have a common bond we must have a common principle. And I beg to premise that it is not in opposition to temperance societies, *as such*, that I may make any remarks which may *seem* hostile to them. On the contrary, I really desire to seek and to find some common principle, on which not merely an humble individual like myself may cooperate with them, but that thousands of the most respectable members of society at large may join their ranks; that hostile clamour may be silenced; that the loud laugh of ridicule may be exchanged for the complacent smile of approbation; and that all pious, sober, and energetic members of the community may unite their efforts in storming the Citadel of Intemperance. I therefore come forward with my designation, that, as the Clergy are called upon in all publications on this subject, we at least may have benefit of a fair and open field. And I avowedly declare my opinions individually, as I think we are all *now* called upon to do, both as a clergyman, and as a member of the community. I do this, as well from the general love of openness and candor, as that—as I have already expressed to you, Sir, in a private letter—on all questions connected with religion and morals I maintain that *high ground*, that of *principle*, should be taken; and to remind those, who so frequently appeal to the Clergy on that *operative* question, if I may so speak, of temperance societies, that we, as the Ministers of Christ, are the proper Guardians of RELIGION in the first place; and that MORALITY must follow in its wake. And it will appear in the sequel of these remarks, if you have patience to bear with the writer of them, that the leading objection to the chief link of temperance societies, namely the " Declaration," is RELIGION. But of this anon.

Your Correspondent, PHILANTHROPOS, writes in a becoming style,—with that moderation of language and manner, by which alone respectful attention can be commanded to any subject whatever. But he skims the surface, rather than dives into the depths of the water. His letter is too general in its remarks to do more than draw the attention of your readers to the question: and that perhaps is all that he proposed to himself in writing it, or that you wished by placing it in your columns. Your last Correspondent, A MEMBER, (I suppose of the Jaffna Temperance Society) has one merit, which Philanthropos has not—he does not *persuade* his friends; but he *dares* certain phantoms, which he has dressed up in the airy habilaments of foes, to the combat. I am certainly no foe to *Temperance!* God forbid that I should be! And while I admire his zeal, and perhaps may smile at his *excessive* earnestness, I own that I do *not* admire the tone and spirit of his letter. I have no taste for that most refined *soubriquet*, (the most objectionable word in our familiar vocabulary) which he iterates, and *re*-iterates, as attaching to temperance societies. I have never called them so, nor in its gross sense have I ever thought them so. My objection is yet more serious, Sir, to his phrase,—the *sense* of which he attributes to yourself,—of " throwing down the *gauntlet* to the Clergy and others of Colombo." There is, says the wise man, a time to speak and a time to keep silence. And your correspondent " comes in such a *questionable* shape that I must speak to him." I will take up his "*gauntlet*," however, in all kindness to his cause, which, in concurrence with him and with you, Sir,

I think the very best. All then, upon which we can be at issue, is the *manner* of conducting this acknowledged good cause. And to show you, Sir, however we may be at issue on this point, that, substantially, I have never been opposed to so good a cause, I find, in a column of my own humble Periodical during the time of its short life, the following account of the introduction of temperance societies into the army.

"The Duke of Wellington has given his sanction to the introduction of temperance societies into the army. In a regimental order of the Grenadier Guards, of which his Grace is Colonel, it is stated that his Grace " has inquired whether any temperance societies exist among them;" and expresses his opinion " of the advantage which might result from the adoption of systematic measures to repress habits of intemperance, and to encourage sobriety"—adding, that " nothing would be wanting in the character of the English Soldier if the prevalent vice of drinking to excess could be eradicated." The order then urges the benefit of temperance, and states " that those who become unfit for the service will receive little or no pension at the examination at Chelsea, if their disability shall be traced to habits of excessive drinking. Such a distinction must be made in justice to the good and steady soldier who preserves his health and serves the proper time."—*Kentish Observer*.

And now, Sir, in reference to the Tracts with which you have kindly favored me, for my better information, as to those societies in which you and your correspondents take so laudable an interest, I have a few words to say. These Tracts consist of " a Complete View of the principles and objects of Temperance Societies by the Rev. John Edgar, Professor of Divinity at Belfast; and of " a Speech of the Rev. J. Maclean, of Sheffield, at the Second Annual Meeting of the British and Foreign Temperance Society held at Exeter Hall, on Tuesday May 22, 1832. The Right Hon. and Right Rev. The Lord Bishop of London in the Chair "

To these you have added the form of, "declaration" which was in 1832 adopted by the British and Foreign Temperance Society, which I shall presently examine, but which I understand has by the American societies been modified, and demands still further modification, I think *nullification*.

At the meeting, referred to in the second Tract, the Bishop of London presided. To that distinguished prelate no one in this island can be more deeply indebted, and, I trust, indelibly grateful, than the writer of this letter. It cannot therefore, and I feel confident it will not, be supposed, for an instant, that I can intend the slightest disrespect to his Lordship, when I comment on a Tract which he may approve, and on the Society to which he has given his powerful countenance and support. He, I am sure, would be the last person who would put such a construction upon what I have written, or may write on the present occasion. I may at the same time take the opportunity to notice the array of high and influential names which is set forth to enforce, as it were, by their reflected light, the arguments of the advocates of Temperance Societies. A good cause does not need the lustre of high names and high characters. It shines by the light of truth itself. Amicus Plato, amicus homo, sed major amica VERITAS. Great names may *illustrate* great truths; but they do not *prove* them. Nor are the Bishop of London, and other distinguished personages, who are members of temperance societies, the authors of, nor accountable for, every part of the system; but they unite with those societies as having a preponderating good, and not as being, what no human system can be, perfect and without spot.

The first Tract lays down the principles of the Societies in these four propositions, which are to be found at the very beginning.

1. "Temperance Societies lay as their foundation two great laws—Christian charity and self preservation. They neither propose to employ a means of reformation superior to the Gospel, nor different from it, but merely to put into practical operation principles which the Gospel has taught.

2. "There is no account, it is true of their establishment, more than of the establishment of Bible or Missionary Societies; but all the principles on which they are founded, and which they teach, are to be found there.

3. "Their object is to produce a great change on public opinion and practice; their instrument for effecting this is not coercion in any form, but simply the truth spoken in love.

4 " Knowing that prevention is better than cure, their desire is to cut off the sources of drunkenness, and these sources they conceive are found in the opinions and practices of the temperate."

1. To the first proprositions, abstractedly, no objection can possibly be made. It bases morality on that, upon which alone it can stand, the Christian Religion.

2. The principle of Bible or Missionary Societies (our Church Societies for promoting Christian Knowledge, and for the Propagation of the Gospel in foreign parts, the oldest Bible and Missionary Societies, might have been named) this principle is surely bound up in the Bible itself, The Bible was written by the inspiration of the Holy Ghost. It was intended to be read by all mankind. It must therefore be dispersed among all nations. St. Paul and the apostles were the first Missionaries.

Temperance is a part only of the great moral law of the Bible, one of the lovely graces of Christianity. And, with reverence I say it, the first and the best temperance societies were unquestionably the Schools of the Prophets and the College of the Apostles, who, like righteous Abel, " being dead yet speak." And if with Felix, when Paul "reasoned of righteousness, *temperance* and judgment to come," unrighteous and intemperate men, do not " tremble," and go further than Felix, by efficacious "repentance not to be repented of,"—I confess that my own hopes of the success of any subsidiary aids are very faint. RELIGION, then, we are agreed, must be the basis of temperance, and of any societies for the promotion of temperance. In such subsidiary expedients, therefore, we must be specially careful not to violate any known law of that religion, for this, or for any other good end.

3. The third proposition, I humbly think is contradicted by the imposition of the DECLARATION,—which is surely the strongest possible *moral* coercion. And yet it is gravely asserted, that whereas " their object is to produce a great change on public opinion and practice"—yet "their instrument for effecting this is not coercion in any form, but simply the truth spoken in love."

4. The last proposition is the master paradox, on which the entire system of temperance societies seems to revolve,— and which, I fear, deters many good people from giving this laudable work their countenance and assistance. It is surely as palpable a solecism as was ever invented by the perverted ingenuity of that ingenious piece of contradiction, the human mind, to affirm, " That the sources of drunkenness are found in the opinions and practices of the temperate; and that they have been the chief agents of promoting and perpetuating drunkenness." It is called, " *a great discovery ;*" and such it undoubtedly is. " *The great discovery,*" says Professor Edgar, *which now flashes across the world with the lightning's brightness, is that the temperate are the chief promoters of drunkenness.*" Now really, Sir, I, in my simplicity, have believed, ever since I was first taught, and understood any thing of my Bible, that the sources of drunkenness, and of every other vice which defiles our nature, are to be found in the corruption of the human heart, and in the depravity of the human will. And surely no isolated instances of temperate persons having unadvisedly and unconsciously strengthened and confirmed this habitual vice in some wretched individuals, can go further than *to prove the general rule,*—but can never undermine the foundation principle, upon which the whole is based.

We are hence led to inquire, 1. into the real sources originating this perilous sin, this wide spread moral contagion at this period; 2. in what grade of Society it is principally, indeed almost exclusively, found; and 3. what is the best remedy. In the process of this inquiry, I shall take occasion to notice such parts of the Tracts as appear to be necessary to our present purpose,—especially the "DECLARATION," which, with the resolutions and rules of the Society, is appended to the Rev. Mr. Maclean's speech.

1. In addition to the common origin to which I have referred, as seated in the hearts of all mankind, of the sin and evil of this bad world,—the existence of the great number of licensed distilleries is the paramount *proximate* cause of the melancholy state of inebriety and depravity which now exists. I will not go so far as to say, with the learned Professor of Divinity, who is the author of the first tract, that, "in suffering distilled spirits at all as an ordinary drink, the world has been the subject of a deception, whose consequences will be felt in the lowest hell." I think that this is too strong language. But the drinking raw spirits, in the form of drams,—especially in tropical climates,—is the most pernicious habit, the most destructive of body and soul, and the deepest injury to society at large, which can possibly be contracted. And the *true* origin of this is, I repeat, the number of licensed distilleries, and the low duties, to the consumer, on ardent spirits, both here and at home. You, Sir, who are jealously watchful over the errors of governments, and a sort of voluntary political guardian,—can you not bend *one* of your Argus' eyes on *this* cause!! Can you not,—by rule upon rule, and line upon line, as we teach children—din into the ears of our Legislators and Governors, that *they* are the chief causes of the existing drunkenness of the common people, and of our fine soldiery, who are ruined and ruining (the work of destruction never stops) by the free access to the arrack shop in our Eastern Colonies, and to the gin and whiskey shops at home Your quiver, Sir, should never be emptied of its arrows, which you should continually discharge against this great cause of the existing evil. You should reverse the poetic maxim.

Neque semper arcum
Tendit Apollo.

Away with the *Neque!* Bend your bow, and shoot your arrows, not like the wicked "privily," but openly, publicly, fearlessly! Temperance societies, and all other means are vain to stem this torment of wickedness and drunkenness, if it be not opposed by the strong hand of Legislation. Hence I admire, I greatly admire, that part of the first tract, which details the acts of legislation from the reign of Louis XII. of France to the middle of the last century, by French and Swedish Kings, as well as by our own Parliaments. And by these means alone will the present tide of drunkenness be arrested. But this brutal vice will never be suppressed, unless and until the Governments of our fine country, and of her numerous colonies, will oppose some strong act of legislation against this predominating sin of a suffering people.

2. The origin of the almost universal prevalence of drunkenness among one class of people is, I think, but too plainly the universal prevalence of cheap spirits. The giant vice is fed from this inexhaustible source for ever :—and until the Government of Great Britain cease to collect its revenue, regardless of the moral wellbeing of the people, this evil will continue. But whence sprang temperance societies? From America. They seem to be levelled against *every* grade of Society. This is a vital error; for however it may be in America, "unbounded intemperance," neither in the use of spirits nor of wine, is not the existing vice of the higher and middle classes of society of our country, "Unbounded intemperance," among ourselves is almost exclusively confined to the lowest grade as a class. Individual instances, of whatever class, I do not contemplate. Yet your first tract states that the member of a temperance society, "evidences by his practice his conviction that the state and taste of society have been grievously vitiated—he withdraws himself from all connection with those opinions and practices by which in the present depraved state of society the use of intoxicating liquor is made essential to health and social intercourse, and from which, as the most prolific of all sources, springs the overwhelming drunkenness of our day." Now I must take the liberty to deny this in toto. The *earthly* origin of the present state of drunkenness is, as I have shown, the easy access of the common people to ardent spirits. *Society,*—as that term is commonly used in application to the higher and middle classes,—was never, from the date of the reign of GEORGE III. to the present moment, and for many years past, more free from this vice among our own countrymen, although it may still admit of further improvement. Our universities, once the hot-beds of excess in every shape, especially of wine, have for at least twenty years and upwards, been surprisingly reformed. For that space of time at least drinking has been looked down upon as an ungentlemanly habit, and those who are guilty of it as ungentlemanly characters. It is the same in the society of gentlemen in private life. Manners have purified morals, and subserved religion. It is, I think, this sweeping attack of temperance societies, indiscriminately, upon every class of the community, which has excited the opposition and the derision,

against which, I deeply lament, the exemplary members of these Societies have had to contend. For this reason they have been opposed or neglected by the most temperate men, whose object, as well as the object of those societies, is emphatically temperance in its most general sense. Our lower grades of society,—our soldiers, and our servants, domestic and public,—these are the present victims of this abhorrent and fatal habit. But unless some modification of temperance society regulations be adopted, I fear that, with all their array of names and numbers, they will have small influence on the aggregate of society, especially in reference to this colony; and that without the suppression of the poison itself, in reference to the whole Empire, the VICE will NEVER be suppressed, as a national vice, a national disgrace, and a national calamity.

3. We now come to the last and most important question:—what is the remedy for this acknowledged, wide-spread, moral pestilence,—the habitual drunkenness of the common people, the most numerous, and, when well guided and governed, the most effective class of mankind. You, Sir, will say, *temperance societies*, as subsidiary to religion, are the best remedy for this evil. And if,—as I have said in the first part of this too long letter,-*some common bond or principle could be found*, in which all friends of religion, of good order, and of temperance, in its most comprehensive sense, could unite, they *might be* extremely beneficial. Temperance societies demand of every individual of their members to subscribe a "DECLARATION;" and the one with which you have favored me, and which professes to be "more simple" than previous ones, is as follows:—"We agree to abstain from distilled spirits, except for medicinal purposes, and to discountenance the causes and practice of intemperance." This declaration, it seems, as I have already noticed, has undergone some modification. I hope, Sir, you will not judge me an intemperate man in the use of strong drinks; but I frankly confess that I could not sign the above with a clear conscience. Indeed I should disapprove of *any* declaration on principles both of prudence and of religion. I think it imprudent in any one, however abstemious his habits, to take upon him this arbitrary vow (for a vow I must consider it). Nor are we told how many, perhaps thousands, who have subscribed their names to these or similar words, have broken their vow through strong temptation;—nor how many of more regular habits, have broken it through inadvertence* I would willingly join to the utmost of my ability in

* In one of your recent Editorial articles, respecting temperance societies you mention the unostentatious efforts which have been made to form one in Colombo. I speak from correct information when I state that, of the numerous

any measures which might, unitedly, by a number of respectable and influential persons, be deemed advisable, " to discountenance the causes and practices of intemperance." And who would not ? But I could not sign such a contract, or declaration. Distilled spirits are used in various forms, culinary as well as medicinal; and I know not any thing which can make a more convenient loophole for equivocation and mental reservation than the word *medicinal* in this form of "declaration." According to the discipline of the Romish Church, as we all know, in Roman Catholic countries particular days are prescribed for fastings which, at certain seasons, such as Lent, are rendered more than ordinarily numerous and severe. I have passed two years of my life in a Roman Catholic country: and I have observed the following evils to arise out of this discipline. The devotees, who rigidly obey their priests, affix to ordinary food an *over*-value which we can scarcely conceive. While others, on the contrary, who are more rich and more lax, evade this abstinence precisely on the principle of the word "medicinal" in your Declaration. "*They have weak stomachs, and cannot bear fasting !!!*"

Spectatum admissi risum teneatis amici?

Will not similar consequences follow total abstinence from all spirituous liquors ? Will they not be over-valued by some; while others will imitate the Roman Catholics, and evade the observance of their vow on the score of health ?

In the suppression of drunkenness, as a necessary and indispensable object, we should have a perfect union of purpose and of principle. But surely it cannot be necessary that, to accomplish this most desirable object, every *temperate* person should be called upon to sign a declaration to abstain totally from that, to the abuse of which he has no sort of temptation. Freedom from such arbitrary pledges should be granted on the principle of the old maxim: Sit in necessariis *unitas*, in non necessariis *libertas*, in omnibus *caritas*. "In things necessary let there be *unity ;* in things not (absolutely) necessary, *liberty;* in all things, *charity*" No improper motives should be imputed to those who support. nor to those who object to temperance societies. Full credit for upright intention should be mutually given and received. The object is desirable by all; in the mode of attaining that object many may differ. But charity should subsist along with liberty of opinion. A higher principle than that of prudence or expediency, may restrain some of the most undoubted, nay even the most powerful friends of so-

individuals who signed that *declaration at least three fourths immediately violated their pledge*: while, on the other hand, some others, of most unexceptionable characters, withdrew their names,—alleging that their health would suffer by total abstinence; and that, in this climate, they required *some* stimulant, however small.

briety, from enrolling their names among the members of temperance societies. Such individuals will feel compelled by
their consciences to follow the guidance of their principles.
Such are my own scruples; and though not among the most
powerful, I claim the humble merit to be among the honest:—
and I candidly confess myself to be of that class, who will
scruple to sign what is called a "Declaration." That declaration assumes, indeed, the form of an agreement or contract. But
to my plain understanding it is substantially of the nature of a
vow, though it bear not the character of a *religious* vow. But
are *any* vows, even religious vows, agreeable to the spirit of
the Christian religion? A vow, without any apparent sanction
of religion, can never be deemed lawfully by any person calling
himself religious. For my own part I question the lawfulness
even of religious vows. Mr. Maclean, in his speech, owns that
conscientious people do object and say, "I conscientiously abstain from spirits; and I do it upon principle; but I cannot sign
your agreement; I cannot make that which in itself is lawfully a
sin." This objection he answers by drawing a comparison between the agreement, professed in the declaration, not to drink
spirits, and ordinary mercantile contracts. I think that there
is no analogy between them. I cannot concede that the temperance declaration *is* of the nature of a contract, or "a mutual agreement," as this gentleman terms it. I maintain, on the
contrary, that it is a *vow*, and not a contract; and that, as a
vow, it is not agreeable to the Christian religion.

A contract is a mutual agreement between two parties upon
an equal footing to do some specific thing, which is in the power
of each contracting party to perform, and which for some valu-
able consideration he undertakes to fulfil. But the declaration
of the temperance society is not between two parties upon an
equal footing: they who agree are all of one party: and who is
of the other? The Supreme Being. Can the contract, I ask, be
fulfilled without, and independent of God? The term contract,
as applied to the declaration, has this impropriety,—that the
subject being a moral law, and the author of that law the Supreme Being, man cannot contract with man respecting that
which appertains to God. Temperance is a moral law bound
upon the conscience of man by God. It needs no additional
obligation to be observed by ourselves, nor enforced upon others:
for nothing can possibly make it more binding than it originally
is. No contract can exist between unequal parties; and it is a
mere fallacy to affirm this declaration to be a contract between
the individuals who sign it: for, as I have already stated, that
which they undertake to perform, respects not themselves as
separate parties, but as one party. The obligation is not to
each other, but to God; and the subject of the contract, as it res-

pects the discountenance of intemperance, has no reference to the contracting parties, but to a *third* party, their fellow creatures, who may be the victims of intemperance. This, too, is the duty of every member of society, and is strictly binding, whether or not it be the subject of any express declaration, contract, or vow. It is also the duty of a religious person as part of his duty to God. The declaration, then, I contend, is not of the nature of a contract; for such a contract, in the nature of things, is impossible.

We can as reasonably and as lawfully contract that our bodies shall henceforth be and continue in a perfect state of health, or that they shall be preserved from any particular disease, as we can undertake that our minds, or souls, shall be henceforth, in whole or in part, sinless and blameless; or that we shall henceforth undeviatingly abstain from any particular sin,—which amounts to the same thing. Both the body and the soul are preserved in existence by the power and by the grace of God,—exercised over the physical health of the body, and over the moral health of the mind, or soul. Over both we possess control to a certain extent, and subject to certain laws. Intemperate indulgence of *any* appetite is certainly injurious to both. But, so far as regards *our* control, we are nothing. The life itself of frail beings, such as we are, is held upon most uncertain tenure: and not being able, in a general sense, to think or to do one good thing without God, we hold, in dependence upon a Higher Power, our mental and moral existence, which, though governed by certain and unerring laws, yet so far as *our* power is concerned, is entirely without and beyond our control. Without the Divine Providence, and the ordinary means of health, we cannot preserve the health of the body; without prayer, and the appointed means of grace, we cannot preserve the moral health of the soul.—As in the days of Christ and the Apostles, evil spirits, or demons, may again have power over our bodies and our souls. We are no where assured that this *temporary* power will not be again permitted. We are only assured,—and we are bound to believe, that Christ has *effectually* and *permanently* " destroyed the works of the Devil,"—so that evil spirits can have no *abiding* power, at least over the faithful: and these awful influences over men, in the time of the Messiah, were undoubtedly permitted, that the superior power of the Redeemer over these fallen spirits, or demons, might be the more triumphantly displayed. As the species of madness, called lunacy, was, in those days, inflicted by demons upon men; so the madness of intoxication, or any other disease, physical or moral, or partaking of both, may, with the powerful aid of our own appetites and passions, be the " work of the Devil," or the suggestion of demons. And, at all events, direct demoniacal possession, or influence, over the bodies and souls of men, *may be* again inflicted upon our world. Indeed, we are far from sure that, as the second Advent of Christ approaches, when the power of the enemy will, it is foretold, be temporarily increased, prior to his utter and final defeat, this power and influence of the apostate band of fallen spirits, or demons, may, for a time, reappear.

But, Sir, while your temperance "declaration" provides, by the word "medicinal," against the accidents of the *bodily* health, no provision is made for the incidental, or other diseases, or weaknesses, to which surely the *mental* or *moral* health is at least equally exposed. The necessity of a physician, implied by the word "medicinal," equally implies our state of dependence, as to the body, upon a higher power. But it is tacitly assumed that the mind or soul, the thinking faculty, is in our own power; and that the moral control over the human will is undisputed. Else, why is the remedy for a moral and physical evil proposed in this *positive* form: "*I agree* to abstain &c;" and not rather,—"With the help of God, and by the grace of the Holy Spirit, *I will endeavour* to abstain?" But in the temperance "declaration" there is not the most remote intimation, nor the slightest insinuation of doubt, that we have not the most absolute controlling power over our own minds and moral faculties,— in one word, over the WILL. The *implied denial of religious control* is as strong as if it had been stated in so many words. That we have a *limited* control over the will, I am the last man to deny. We are so formed by our gracious Creator; and this control had been perfect, but for the original sin wrought by the defection of our first parents.* Did we not yet possess a *limited* control, we were the blind victims of chance, necessity, fate, predestination, or any other idol principle,—or rather misbegotten phantom assuming the form of a principle,—which that idol-loving thing, the human mind, may set up. But this control *is*

* After arguing in his fine and profound manner, " that obedience of creatures unto the law of Nature is the stay of the whole world,"—the judicious Hooker thus states the partial counteraction of that law :—" Which defect in matters of things natural, they who gave themselves unto the contemplation of Nature amongst the heathen, observed often: *but the true original cause thereof, divine malediction, laid for the sin of man, upon these creatures,* which God made for the use of man, this being an article of that saving truth which God hath revealed unto his Church, was above the reach of their merely natural capacity and understanding. But howsoever these swervings are now and then incident unto the cause of Nature; nevertheless, so constantly the laws of nature are by natural agents observed, that no man denieth, but those things which nature worketh are wrought either always or for the most part, after one and the same manner. If here it be demanded, what this is which keepeth nature in obedience to human law, we must have recourse to that HIGHER LAW, whereof we have already spoken." Eccl. Pol B l. § 3. If this " divine malediction" be passed on the *natural* world, religious persons do not want to be told that it has much more strongly affected the *moral* world. And if to discover that which "keepeth" the moral world at all, however imperfectly, " in obedience to human law we must have recourse to the HIGHER LAW," equally must we have recourse to "that higher law," both for the knowledge and the cure of " defect in the matter of things moral." This, and this only, is the thing "medicinal" to moral "defect;" and this, and this only, is entirely lost sight of in the temperance " declaration."

limited. If it so please God, all power of self-control may be momentarily taken from the best of men: and such self-control, as a judicial punishment, *is* taken from the abandoned; as we see exemplified in those very victims of drunkenness, upon whom, Sir, you call, as having perfect possession of their minds, and controlling power over their wills, to sign your " Declaration," at which better men " start up alarmed." Our self control is, evidently, *conditional* upon our use or abuse of it. The two contrary extremes, into which the human mind falls,—and, me—thinks, I have observed the *same* mind, at different periods, and under different circumstances, actuated by both these extremes,—are, the abandonment of *all* control from above, which I maintain to be the tendency of your " Declaration;" or to be tied down, as it were, hand and foot, without *any* controlling power over the will, by the phantom principles which I have named,—and which, like the Golden Calves at Bethel and at Dan, are set up in the human heart by some momentary predominating passion, or impulse, in the place of sober truth. But they bear no more true resemblance to the serene and steady light of truth, than the broad and diffused light of the sun at midday, is like.

> " The brief and collied lightning in the night,
> Which ere a man hath power to say, Behold,
> The jaws of darkness do devour it up."

If then this " declaration" be not,—as I think I have proved to demonstration,—of the nature of a *contract*, it must assume the form and character of a *religious vow;* and it only remains that we examine into the lawfulness, or the unlawfulness of vows, according to the Christian religion.

Vows were permitted to the Jews, and form a part of their discipline. The Mosaic dispensation was, however, imperfect; and many things were by it enjoined and permitted, which were done away by the Gospel. Our inquiry, therefore, is whether any and what vows are prescribed by the Christian dispensation. In the New Testament two sorts of vows are mentioned or implied,—general and particular. Our baptismal obligations are, in the first place, of the nature of vows, by our sponsors, before we are able to take them upon ourselves; when they cease to be vows, and become obligations.—Of particular vows we meet with two instances in the New Testament. Both have reference to the discipline of the Mosaic law. Both respect the vow of Nazaritism prescribed, Numb. 6. 18—21. The first was made at Cenchrea. Acts. 18. 18. But whether it was made by St. Paul or Aquila, commentators are not agreed. Nor is it of the slightest importance. The second (Acts. 21. 23.) was made by St. Paul at Jerusalem, as a matter of expediency, not of necessity; by the advice of the Jewish Christians, and to conciliate converts of that nation. For the same reason St. Paul " circumcised Timothy because of the Jews;" though he expressly declared (Gal. 5. 6.) That " in Jesus Christ neither circumcision availeth any thing nor uncircumcision: but faith which worketh by love."—I shall cite two passages, from two celebrated commentators of different denominations, in illustration of each of these texts. On the first, Whitby a divine of the Church of England, says,— " There was in the vow of the Nazarites a moral part, namely, the consecration of themselves to God, and to a greater degree of purity; and in this, Christians might comply with it without scruple; and it had a ceremonial part, the cutting off the hair, and the offering sacrifices when it was accomplished; and as to this, St. Paul and other Christians, knowing that the law was not obligatory, might dispense with themselves; omit, or do them, as prudence and the case of scandal did require. For though St. Paul went up now to Jerusalem, we read not of any offering that he made according to the law, nor perhaps would he have shaved his head on this account, had not some scrupulous Jews at Corinth, been conscious to his vow."—The other commentator, the late celebrated Dr. Adam Clarke, concludes his note on the vow of St. Paul at the temple at Jerusalem in these remarkable words: "Indeed, *vows* rather referred to a *sense of obligation*, and the *gratitude* due to God for mercies already received, than to the procuring of future favors of any kind. Besides, God had not yet fully shown that the law was abolished; he tolerated it till the time that the iniquity of the Jews was filled up; and then, by the destruction of Jerusalem he swept every rite and ceremony of the Jewish law away, with the besom of destruction."*

According, then, to the Christian religion vows appear to be unlawful. There is no warranty for them in the New Testament; and the abuse of them by heathens, and by Christian churches, in which they are retained as a part of discipline, fully establishes their abolition to be scriptural. The providence of God, visible to the eye of faith in the affairs of the world, is the safest possible commentary on the Scriptures. Vows are, I believe, universal among heathen nations: and whence are derived the vows of celibacy in the Romish Church,—so fruit-

* As so many names are brought forward in support of temperance societies, it is but fair to state the opinion of Dr. Adam Clarke respecting them. His piety and worth are too well known to need mention. By principle and by habit he was remarkably abstemious; he drank wine most sparingly, and seldom used spirits, except medicinally. Yet *he* was decidedly opposed to the vow of temperance societies upon religious principles.

ful of evil both moral and political,—but from the vestal vows of the ancient Romans? Any thing, therefore, which partakes of the nature of a vow,—and such I think I have proved the declaration of temperance societies to be,—ought surely to be studiously avoided and discountenanced. At least it is not the duty of the Clergy, who have been so repeatedly called upon, Sir, by you and your correspondents, to promote even so righteous an end as temperance and sobriety, by means which they conscientiously believe, not only to have no warranty in the Holy Scriptures, but to be tacitly forbidden by those inspired oracles.

It were imposible for any one drawn into the close contact and connection with the soldiery,—into which, especially by the bedside of the sick and the dying, it is the lot of the Clergy to be drawn,—without observing, I may say, with

> "a watchful heart.
> Still couchant, an inevitable ear,
> And an eye practised like a blindman's touch,"—

not to feel, in a word, with the deepest sensibility, the melancholy state of inebriety in which they are almost hopelessly immersed,—and not to be actuated by the strongest desire to rescue them from the gulph of moral depravity, into which they have desperately plunged, and in which they lie blindly wallowing. This is strong language, but not too strong to depict the unhappy degradation of our gallant soldiers by a solitary vice. To remedy this dreadful and widespread evil, however, something must be resorted to far more comprehensive and more efficacious than the *panacea* of the much lauded temperance societies.—Deeply therefore as, in common with every one,—and especially in my capacity of a Military Chaplain,—I feel and deplore the melancholy state of inebriety at which the common people, especially the private soldiers, have arrived; frequently as I find it necessary, both in my public and private ministrations,—particularly in the military hospital,—to deprecate this odious vice in the strongest terms which my feelings may suggest, and which my powers of utterance enable me to select (and I may appeal to my brethren, the soldiers, whom I have had occasion to address in the hospital, whether it be not a *very* frequent subject of my earnest and affectionate warnings and exhortations to them) I cannot, with a clear conscience, unite with the temperance societies on their present system. I cannot honestly and religiously sign such a *votive* declaration myself; I cannot recommend to others that which, as a Christian, I deem unlawful,— and as a member of society,—notwithstanding the imposing reports and pamphlets of these societies,—I believe to be in the highest degree perilous. *I know* but one instance; and that I have already named. That respects the society of Colombo; and that has failed in this most vulnerable part. Religious persons, I apprehend, incur danger by taking upon them so rash a vow. The profligate rushes heedlessly upon destruction. In the first storm of temptation his good resolutions are overwhelmed and forgotten; his hopes of the future are wrecked; his vows, like those of the Poet's ship-wrecked mariner in the Ionian sea, are buried in the waters of oblivion; and his dependence on a higher Power, like the tutelary gods carved on the heathen vessel, are cast upon the shore of destruction.

> Trabe rupta Bruttia saxa
> Prendit amicus inops, remque omnem surdaque vota
> Condidit Ionio: jacet ipse in litore, et una
> Ingentes de puppe dei, jamque obvia mergis
> Costa ratis laceroe. *Persius* Sat. vi. 27.

> "A friend, scarce rescued from the Ionian wave,
> Grasps a projecting rock, while, in the deep,
> His treasures, with his vows, unheeded sleep:
> I see him stretched, desponding, on the ground,
> His tutelary gods all wrecked around,
> His bark dispersed in fragments o'er the tide,
> And sea-mews sporting on the ruins wide."

GIFFORD.

If it be practicable, consistently with the object of these societies, to do away with this declaration; if resolutions be drawn by a select and friendly committee, in which *all* persons can unite; if a meeting be called, to which, after due deliberation, these resolutions may be safely proposed,—and subscriptions entered into for providing a wholesome substitude for ardent spirits,—I will render my humble assistance with the greatest pleasure and alacrity. I will join, heart and hand, in so praiseworthy, and so noble an undertaking, as the attempt to rescue our suffering fellow creatures from the certain destruction of intemperance.

I have now, Sir, only to apologize to you for taking up so much of your space and time, which might be better employed; and to the public, for intruding upon them on this subject. I have done it with unfeigned reluctance. But as I am the Chaplain stationed at Colombo; as my duties are greatly military; and as the Clergy of Colombo in particular have been so repeatedly invited to come forward,—I should have deemed it an unmanly dereliction of my Christian duty, after having given the question my most attentive consideration, to have shrunk from the candid declaration of my sentiments.

I am, Sir,
Your obedient servant.

Colpetty
Sep. 29. 1835.   THE SENIOR COLONIAL CHAPLAIN.

APPENDIX.

APPENDIX

Since the foregoing letter was written, and while it was passing through the press, I have been favored with some particulars respecting the attempt to establish a Temperance Society at the station of Galle. I do not make the statement of facts as being quite *authentic;* but I believe they will be found to be generally correct. Where they are incorrect, I shall be happy to be set right; for my sole desire is, to give a statement of *facts,* upon which the Public may rely.

The attempt failed, I understand, even more than at Colombo. Few, if any, of the officers, and other respectable inhabitants joined it. It was established at the latter end of 1834, and ceased, I am informed, on or about January 1835. A *very* limited number of the private soldiers joined it: and not all of these,— I know not what proportion,—adhered to the vow. As substitutes for spirits, wine and beer were provided. Of the proximate cause of its cessation altogether—perhaps the removal of the detachment—I am not accurately informed. But the *true* causes of its meeting with nothing approaching to success, at any period of its short life, were evidently those which have been insisted on in the foregoing pages. Arrack, it seems, is greatly cheaper at Galle than at Colombo; and to incite the poor victims further, effervescent toddy, to mix with it, to an unlimited extent, is given *gratis.* The other, and still stronger cause, I think, is the *declaration,* or vow; for the following, which is A FAC-SIMILE, is surely a vow:—

I   *solemnly*

promise and engage myself that for the next months ensuing or until I give at least a weeks notice to the Chaplain or to some person appointed by him to receive the same, I will abstain from the use of ardent spirits altogether unless strictly for medicinal purposes when I will report my having done so and mention the quantity employed. And moreover I engage to the best of my ability to discourage the use of ardent spirits among my Comrades except in cases of the like nature.

The above is not a declaration, nor is it in the *form* of a contract, but a most solemn personal promise or vow; and, as far as it is intelligible, of the most dangerous kind. The limit of the period is exactly that which meets the superstitious notions of the depraved soldier, who will make oath, vow, or promise for any period, so that that period be limited. This fact will, I think, be attested by every officer in His Majesty's service. In Ireland, I have been told, and probably elsewhere, this vow is known by a profane, and vulgar appellation; and that at the end of the period, if the vow be kept, the unhappy victim commits the most abhorrent excess, which, in some instances, has been known to terminate in almost instantaneous death.

So much for the *south* of the island. With what success the temperance societies have been formed in the *north*, I have not been able to ascertain; although I have lately had the pleasure of partially perusing the second number of "The Oriental Temperance Advocate" for July 1835. I find in it, among some very unmeaning maxims, the following: "I never have seen a devoted, intelligent, warm hearted Christian opposed to temperance societies." Before this writer of maxims had ventured on so sweeping denunciation of all his brethren of the Christian faith, who are so unfortunate as to differ with him, and others, on this "*most important topic that has been agitated in modern times,*"* he might have remembered the following *maxim,* the authority of which is indisputable: " Now the end of the commandment is CHARITY out of a pure heart, and of a *good con-*

---

* See the Colombo Observer's leading article 15th September 1835.

science, and of *faith unfeigned.*"‡   We may surely be "devoted and warm hearted Christians," and, so far as the knowledge of our duty goes, "intelligent," without being enrolled among the members of the Jaffna, or of any other temperance society. Nay, we may have *religious scruples,* which *may* issue out " of a *good conscience,* and of *faith unfeigned.*"   By such language, as is used by the *temperate* writer of these maxims, temperance societies cannot be made conducive to a good and Christian end.   We must first "*temper* our own thoughts with *charity.*" There are more kinds of *intemperance* than the *bodily* excess of ardent spirits.   The *mind* may be *distempered* with uncharitableness. We must not impute evil motives, nor detract from any one's character, moral, religious, or intellectual, if we hope to reap the harvest of moral good.

Another of these maxims is: " I have never seen an opposer of temperance societies, who could give any *substantial reason* for his opposition."   I have given *some* reasons against the present constitution of temperance societies: but whether they be *substantial* or not, the Public will judge.

While the foregoing sheets were in the progress of printing, I have also had the opportunity, and the sincere pleasure, of perusing three additional tracts on the question of temperance societies.   1. An excellent speech of the Lord Bishop of London, on the opening of the meeting, at which he presided, in 1832,—and at which Mr. Maclean's speech was likewise delivered.   2. A speech, of much eloquence and acuteness, by P. C. Crampton Esq. at the first public meeting of the British and Foreign Temperance Society in London in 1831.   And 3. A letter of P. C. Crampton Esq. to Dr. Harvey, honorary secretary to the Hibernian temperance society, in answer to objections to the declaration.   As all these tracts,—together with the tract of Professor Edgar, which has been already noticed,— will, I understand, be reprinted, much need not be said respecting them.   But I must frankly confess,—with my deepest respect and veneration for the Right Reverend President, and with my unaffected admiration of the ingenuity and eloquence of the then Solicitor General (I hope now a Judge) for Ireland,— that my feelings respecting the declaration are unchanged.

These tracts affectingly describe the alarming state to which intoxication has reduced the lower orders of people in Great Britain and Ireland.   We know to what a dangerous extent it exists in the Tropics.   *Something must be done!*   But will the present and proposed temperance societies admit of no improvement, of no modification?   Are they as perfectly formed, as Minerva sprang from the head of Jove?   Are their rules as unalterable as the laws of the Medes and Persians? May

---

‡ 1. Tim, 1, 5.

they not, in their details at least, admit of some modifications, which may make them more suitable to tropical climates? Cannot the declaration, which is unchangeable by climate.—

Cælum non animum mutant qui trans mare currunt—

be modified, or done away? I have been recently informed (and the information is derived from the lately arrived Missionaries) that difficulties are springing up even in America, its birth-place, respecting the declaration. The main objection, adduced in the foregoing pages, is not directly *met* in any of these tracts. It is indeed slightly touched, and then left by Mr. Crampton, who, thus concludes his letter to Dr. Harvey, with an air of triumph:—Let the religious man,—if any such doubt the propriety of the pledge we demand,—let the religious man ask his own conscience, why it was that the special favor of the Most High seems ever to have accompanied the Nazarite's vow of abstinence, and why it is that "Jonadab the son of Rechab shall not want a man to stand before the Lord for ever." This is a specious and a confident appeal. But the answers to these questions are very simple. 1. The Nazarites' vow was a *religious* vow, *prescribed* by the law of Moses. The declaration, demanded by temperance societies, is not, and professes not to be *religious;* and if it be made religious, it is no where *prescribed* in the New Testament. Roman Catholic vows were among the first corruptions, against which the heroic Luther declaimed: nor ought we to clog the Protestant faith with unnecessary vows. 2. The divine promise to the son of Rechab, was not in reward of the abstinence from wine of himself and his family, any more than because they did not "build houses, nor sow seed, nor plant vineyards, nor have any; but all their days dwelt in tents" until compelled to take refuge at Jerusalem.—The divine promise was in reward of *obedience to a divine law,*—the fifth commandment of the Decalogue:— "Honour thy father and thy mother, *that thy days may be long in the land which the Lord thy God giveth thee.*" When therefore the "pots full of wine, and cups," were "set before the sons of the house of the Rechabites,"—"they said, we will drink no wine: *for Jonadab the son of Rechab our father commanded us, saying, ye shall drink no wine, neither ye, nor your sons for ever"*—"*Thus have we obeyed the voice of Jonadab the son of Rechab our father,* in all that he charged us, to drink no wine all our days, we, our wives, our sons, nor our daughters." The prophet then contrasts the obedience of these pious sons and daughters of Rechab to the command of their earthly father, with the impiety and disobedience of "Judah and the inhabitants of Jerusalem" towards their heavenly father. The blessing upon the Rechabites therefore immediately follows the denunciation upon Judah and Jerusalem. "And Jeremiah said unto the house of the Rechabites thus saith the Lord of Hosts, the God of Israel; *because ye have obeyed the commandment of Jonadab your father, and kept all his precepts, and done according to all that he hath commanded you:* THEREFORE thus saith the Lord of Hosts, the God of Israel, Jonadab the son of Rechab shall not want a man to stand before me for ever." (Jeremiah xxxv.)

The objection to *our* objections are not, therefore, so formidable as they appear. They are indeed no objections whatever. But may it be asked, in conclusion, why the Temperance Societies may not, like the Societies for Promoting Christian Knowledge, and for the Propagation of the Gospel,—and the Bible and Missionary Societies,—be associations of persons, bound together by certain rules and regulations; and confirmed by subscriptions of money? This suggestion is thrown out with all respect and good will to individuals, who are most desirous to establish a temperance society in Colombo: and that the writer of these remarks may not have the character of nothing *but* an objector, he begs to suggest some regulations, like the following, as not altogether unworthy the consideration of these gentlemen:—

1. That a subscription be entered into for providing a substitute for ardent spirits, for the use of private soldiers, and others who cannot afford to buy wine and beer at their present prices.

2. That the stock of wine and beer be placed under the superintendence of some trustworthy persons; under certain regulations; and sold out at reduced prices, and in stated quantities.

3. That a rate of subscription be fixed, both for the more opulent classes who voluntarily contribute to this good work; and likewise for private soldiers, and others, according to their means, but to be fixed so low as that it shall be an obvious gain and privilege to such persons.

4. That none of the poorer classes, private soldiers and others, will be entitled to such privilege who do not subscribe; and that their subscription shall constitute them members of the society, and subject to its laws,—the chief of which shall be *abstinence from spirits as a beverage.*

5. That donations, independent of subscriptions, be not only received, but earnestly entreated, from the more opulent members of society.

6. That a select committee be formed to make laws and by-laws; but that no subscription to a declaration be required of any member of THE PROPOSED COLOMBO TEMPERANCE SOCIETY.—

SUBSTANCE OF A SPEECH,

DELIVERED AT A PUBLIC MEETING HELD AT COLOMBO, FOR THE

FORMATION OF THE CEYLON TEMPERANCE SOCIETY,

ON SATURDAY FEBRUARY 6TH 1836.

THE HONBLE. MR. JUSTICE NORRIS, PRESIDENT.

BY THE SENIOR COLONIAL CHAPLAIN

OF THE ISLAND OF CEYLON.——

(CTEDEXTRA FROM THE COLOMBO OBSERVER.
FEBRUARY 16th 1836.)

~~~~~~~~

The REV. B. BAILEY, *Senior Colonial Chaplain* spoke in the following manner, in proposing the 5th Resolution.

MR. PRESIDENT.

In rising Sir, to propose the motion, which has been entrusted to me this evening, I feel called upon to make some prefatory observations upon the general objects of the institutions, one of which is about to be more fully established in this Colony, and in explanation of the part I have taken on the present occasion.

It is known that I have written and published a Pamphlet on Temperance Societies,—plainly stating certain objections which I entertained against the old system, but declaring that, so far from opposing Temperance Societies, *as such*, my sole desire was to find some common principle on which myself, and I believed others, could conscientiously co-operate with them. My great and paramount objection was against the DECLARATION required of every member of these societies to be signed and recorded. My objection was founded chiefly on religious grounds. I regarded, and I still regard, this declaration to be of the nature of a vow. I did not feel myself conscientiously at liberty to record such a vow. I could not recommend it to others. I deemed it contrary to the principles and the spirit of Christianity, and highly dangerous in a practical point of view. I hold the same opinion still. My reasons are on record. I need not now enter into them. It is the more particularly unnecessary to do so on the present occasion, because the former things are past away. The old declaration is not required by the gentlemen who have laid the corner stones of the *Ceylon Temperance Society*. I have therefore, as in consistency I was bound, joined it; and I strongly and earnestly recommend others to join it. The simple penalty of infraction of the terms of the Society is now *expulsion*. Nothing that resembles a vow, nothing that binds the conscience with any thing like the obligation of an oath, is now demanded of a subscribing member. Expulsion, however, is no slight penalty. It is an open degradation, and deep disgrace, but not an indelible one. No one ought to sign the resolutions of membership without due consideration. Yet there is nothing in the terms of these resolutions which involves the dangerous moral consequences of a broken vow, or a forfeited oath. Perjury and desperation are not in our train. A vow, or an oath, when once recorded, stands for ever. To break it sinks the moral being irrecoverably, in his own eyes, as well as in the eyes of others. It promises no redemption. And that I have not overdrawn these practical dangers, permit me, before I end this subject, to read a paragraph of an English Newspaper recently put into my hands.

"On Thursday, an inquest was held at the King George public house, Chelsea, on the body of Dennis Carter, aged 38, late a mate of an East Indiaman. Since the return of the deceased from his last voyage, he addicted himself to drinking. Meeting with a Bible a little while ago, he was struck with his bad conduct, and in it wrote the words as follow:—"I promise from this day never to drink grog or blaspheme the name of the Almighty. Dennis Carter." In a very short time his passion for liquor overcame his resolution, and on Tuesday last he got intoxicated; next morning he was sadly grieved at having broken his vow, and the circumstance appeared to prey on his mind. In the evening he cut his throat. Verdict, insanity."—

This needs no comment. Any thing which approaches the *verge* of such a moral precipice, such a possible catastrophe, is surely to be avoided. By the principles of the Ceylon Society such a perilous contingency is struck from the record.

In contemplating the probable good to be derived from such an institution as the one proposed, I would crave a few moments of your attention. One or two difficulties have been urged; but I think they admit of mitigation at least, if not of entire solution. The *possibility* of good has never been denied. The *practicability* is, however, doubted by persons, I hope not otherwise unfavorable to such institutions. There *are* difficulties, which have been felt, and must be felt by all persons who think at all on the subject.

Two difficulties I have myself seen forcibly stated. One is the *inequality of the terms* of the Society demanded of the comparatively rich man and the positively poor man. The richer member, it is said, can use wine, and other beverages, which are beyond the reach of the poorer man. The fact cannot be denied. The other alleged difficulty is the *total* abstinence from spirits in any form, however diluted with water, which, it is contended, is not only harmless, but beneficial. These are confessedly difficulties. But are they insuperable? I think not. Is it not better, at all events, however, to enter the field boldly against a common enemy, though our forces be clogged with certain specific difficulties, than to abandon the field altogether, to be ravaged at will and without resistance? Let us consider these difficulties.

As to the inequality of terms,—I confess that it is a difficulty. I have felt this difficulty. I still feel this difficulty. I proposed a remedy for it, in the shape of *substitution*. But I find that others, whose opinions and experience I am bound to respect, while they have readily met and obviated my principal and paramount objection touching the declaration, still adhere to the general feeling that it is less difficult, on the whole, to let this inequality of worldly circumstances (whence arises the inequality of terms of the Society) take its course among other apparently unequal dispensations of Divine Providence, than to allow of a slight and gradual relaxation of a perilous habit which leads to known and fatal consequences. I own that, as far as I know, from whatever cause, substitution has not yet succeeded. And it is unquestionable that to him who feels the habit of intemperance in the use of intoxicating liquors to have wound its almost inextricable serpent-folds around his very existence, *total abstinence* is the easiest, perhaps the only cure.

Our strife, however, is not against the *temperate use*, but against the *intemperate abuse* of the good gifts of God's Providence. And it is for those individuals, who feel conscious that they have not attained to established habits of temperance and sobriety, to consider whether it were not more desirable to abandon the use of ardent spirits altogether, though they should not be able to furnish themselves with other things, than to peril both body and soul by partaking at all of that which cannot be partaken of without such danger.

But it is objected, whatever the earth produces,—whether spontaneously or under preparation, as distilled spirits,—cannot be deemed essentially hurtful. This may be granted. The

earth's spontaneous produce, and the product of science, such
as distillization, are unquestionably and equally the gift of that
Omniscient God who is as much the Author of the *mind* which
produces science, as of the *earth* which produces corn and
vines. But the necessity for some such remedy as that proposed recurs, under existing circumstances, as strongly when all
this is fully and freely granted. The corruption of the world is
so great,—the appetites and passions of men have such predo-
minance over reason and religion, that some of the stronger
preparations of the produce of the earth,—such as distilled
spirits,—become, under certain circumstances, so pernicious by
their *abuse*, that it is the wisest course to abandon their *use*
altogether. At this moment do we not feel (or why are we
here?) that such an evil exists? The addiction to ardent spirits over the whole British Empire,—owing to their pernicious
cheapness and easy accessibility,— prevails to an alarming, an
extraordinary, an unnatural extent. This Colony, alas! is not ex-
empt from the contagion. The object, therefore, of *all* Temperance Societies, and assuredly of this, is to meet this extraordinary case of difficulty. It is not to stigmatize any of God's creatures of meat or drink. It is not to deny the *uses*, it is to correct
the *abuses* of them. On this ground, I think, the Temperance
Societies are justified in their exclusion of every thing which can
possibly readmit the common enemy into the strong hold of men's
resolutions. The guard is, that in doing so they do not violate any principle of duty, commensurate or superior to the
duty, namely Temperance, to be enforced. Having done away
with the declaration, I humbly think that no paramount objection remains, which ought to prevent, or deter, any one from af-
fording his humble efforts in carrying into effect the necessary
and unexceptionable objects of such associations. I have myself publicly declared my *insuperable* objection to the old system. That objection has been done away. I feel bound as
publicly to declare my abandonment of all *further* and *minor*
objections, as obstacles to my uniting my weak efforts, on the
present occasion, to those of the respectable individuals, who
have begun that which we are now met to extend and to establish,-THE CEYLON TEMPERANCE SOCIETY.

Let me add one word as to the *total* abstinence from ardent
spirits, and the denial of the use of them even in a diluted
form. To such of us as are blessed by Providence with the
means of providing other beverages, surely this is *no* difficulty
and no hardship. Surely, if the terms of this association require it, *we* may dispense with the use of spirits. We may
make this most small sacrifice to the moral well being and happiness of our more unhappy fellow creature, if it have the

most remote influence upon his self-control and self-determination, by the grace of God, to overcome so dreadful a habit.—To him who has been in the habit of drinking raw spirits, or drams, I would address myself with all tenderness and affection, yet with great earnestness; and I would seriously ask him, who has long felt himself enthralled by this perilous habit, whether he can trust *himself* with the taste of spirits, even in a diluted form? And it is on this principle, arising out of the known constitution of our common and frail nature, that the advocates of Temperance Societies, urge, and reasonably urge, *total abstinence.*

The question, I think, resolves itself into this. Are the objections, the inseparable evils and difficulties, of the proposed modified association in this island, paramount to the universal evil, the moral pestilence of the inebriety of the lower classes of people,—the rapid demoralization of all who are involved in this calamitous sin? I think not. I cannot think that any one will seriously affirm it. Is it not better then,—is it not our imperative duty (I now address myself to the higher classes of this assembly) as far as our respective influence extends, to make use of such means as are within our reach,—however imperfect those means may be,—of stemming the torrent, of arresting the downward course of the universal deluge of moral profligacy, which this vice must inflict upon the common people, —and of the injury which it must inflict, and does already inflict upon society generally.

The Temperance Societies are at hand. They have obtained a hold on the common mind. The very prejudices of the people are enlisted in their favor. Modified as the one now proposed is, no *danger* can possibly result to the principles of the parties who engage in it. There may be inconveniences. But there must be certain good, and to a greater extent than we perhaps imagine.

And now, my good friends, and soldiers, let me say a few words to you, for whose benefit particularly I am here this evening, and for whose situation I feel with all kindness and compassion,—but, believe me, without one spark of unkind, rigid and intolerant feeling. I would, however, be understood likewise to address all, without exception, who feel that they have culpably and dangerously indulged in the immoderate use of ardent spirits, until they find the dreadful habit almost, if not altogether, irresistible. But I repeat that I would more particularly address myself to the soldiers. With them I am chiefly connected. I am, soldiers, your chaplain, your clergyman, and, let me add,— for such is my feeling,—I am YOUR FRIEND! I do not come an austere man, a rigid censor, to pass judgment upon you. God forbid! We are all sinful and frail creatures. We must all stand before the judgment seat of Christ. Before that dread tribunal I must answer not only for myself, but for *you*. I must give account of my stewardship in regard to your immortal souls. Hear, therefore, with patience and kind forbearance, the few words I address to you. I come to assist you in a great strait,—to speak to you as friend to friend,—to warn you of the evil of your ways,—but to do this with kindness and with affection. I would moreover point out to you, if practicable, both general and particular ways and means by which you may escape from this dark, dreadful and bewildering path, into a straight way and a good,—cheered by the day-spring from on high,—comforted with the soothing prospect of happiness and repose. Need I!—I need not—remind you of the wretchedness and misery of indulging in the pernicious habit of spirit-drinking, until body and soul, health and happiness, religion and reason fall victims to your fatal inebriety. The loss of life is much and justly insisted on, among the inevitable perils which surround the intemperate spirit-drinker, especially in these climates. And the loss of life, attributable to this sole cause, is great, my friends, among yourselves. Over how many of your comrades have I performed the last solemn service of religion! They are gone! Not a shadow, not a vestige is left of them. They are gone! in early youth,—in prime manhood,—green as the sod which covers their untimely graves. But why and how have they gone? Have they not fallen the victims to that fatal propensity, to save you from which we are met this evening.

But the loss of life, great as it is, is not the greatest evil. The greatest, the most appalling evil is the demoralizing effect of this vicious habit upon the *living* victim. It is the absorption of the spirit of a glorious immortality in one earthly and odious vice. It is the hardening of the heart,—the extinction of the *life of life*, of the faith and hope of a blessed *hereafter*, while the being lingers in a miserable existence *here*. The comforts and consolations of religion flee before him. He stifles his faith. He extinguishes his hope. He destroys his reason. He makes his appetites his masters,—passion the lord of the ascendant. If he think, it is but a moment, to tremble at the abyss yawning beneath his feet ;—and he rushes to the spirit-shop to cast a momentary cloud over his conscience.

I will add no more than to entreat of you, my friends, to pause and think. With all this tide of misery flowing towards you, around you, before you, *within* you, will you not seize any thing rather than put in peril your immortal souls, and render your danger yet more near and unavoidable, by at the same time destroying your earthly existence, and hastening to the grave and —to JUDGMENT !

As an auxiliary to Temperance Societies, it is now my pleasing duty to advert to the Resolution which I am called on to move this evening. I have already said, and I repeat, my friends and soldiers, that I come not to you as a rigid and austere censor, but I address you as your clergyman, and therefore as your *friend!* I know something of human nature. I have lived more than forty years in the world; and I have learned at least one truth, namely, that it is unwise, as well as uncharitable, to take away any thing positive, and to put nothing in its place. There is *one* thirst which you may easily and harmlessly enjoy, under our direction,—*the thirst of knowledge!* Temperance Coffee Houses, and Reading Rooms have been adopted, in aid of Temperance Societies, and have succeeded both in England and India. I have read of a successful one at Madras. We would establish such a room here. It was my suggestion: and the Committee have kindly indulged me with the privilege of proposing this motion. Soldiers, especially in this climate, have much spare time on their hands, which it is not very easy to dispose of. This may have led them to the arrack-shop: and they have continued to " put an enemy into their mouth to steal away their brains" until scarcely any are left to guard the citadel. I would point out a means by which you may recover your scattered powers of understanding.—Abandon the arrack-shop. Join this Society. And step into a room, which, I trust, will be presently prepared for you,—furnished with news-papers and books,—open all day, and lighted up at night. You will soon contract new habits, and enjoy new and innocent pleasures, while you store your minds with instruction. You will then have reason to bless the hour you joined this Society, at which, in your lighter moments, you have laughed, perhaps with scorn. You will lay up stores of *future* happiness, while you are reaping the fruits of *present* temperate and religious enjoyment.

I scarcely, I think, need urge on the higher classes of this assembly the propriety of their contributing to this good work. I have already conversed with some gentlemen of the Colony on the subject,—especially, and most frequently, Soldiers, with your General, who in this, as in all other matters, is your fast and kind friend. He will, I know, contribute, both by donation, and subscription; and I entreat all who are here to follow such example, according to their means,—and to use their influence with others who are absent. A donation will be first required, to meet the first expenses,—and a small monthly subscription afterwards, for furnishing news-papers, periodical publications, and lights. All will be under the management of the Committee.

I may add that there might be also another room in the Pettab, which might be provided by their own contributions, with the addition of voluntary contributions of other benevolent persons.

And now I beg to move the following resolution:

"That there be established a READING ROOM *for the exclusive use of the Members of this Society;* that measures be forthwith adopted to raise funds both by subscription and donations; and that the Committee be authorized to hire a Room for the purpose, to be supplied with Colonial and other news-papers, and periodical publications.

"That every member of this Society, who frequents the Reading Room, pay a monthly subscription of not less than one fanam."

NO 5 58

COLOMBO :—*Printed at the Wesleyan Mission Press.*